THE
Archive Photographs
SERIES

WHITSTABLE

A pathway called Sea Wall, which separates the Horsebridge and Ludgate Hill.

THE
Archive Photographs
SERIES

WHITSTABLE

Compiled by
Mick Glover

CHALFORD

First published 1998
Copyright © Mick Glover, 1998

The Chalford Publishing Company
St Mary's Mill, Chalford,
Stroud, Gloucestershire, GL6 8NX

ISBN 0 7524 1112 8

Typesetting and origination by
The Chalford Publishing Company
Printed in Great Britain by
Bailey Print, Dursley, Gloucestershire

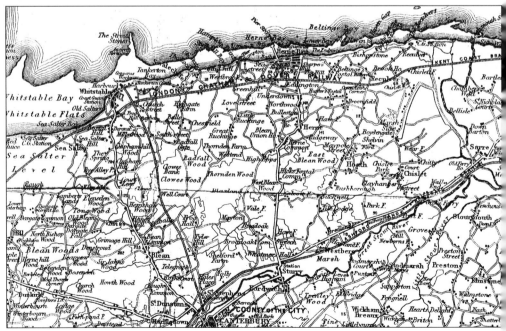

A late nineteenth-century map showing Whitstable and surrounding areas.

Contents

Acknowledgements

A large proportion of the postcards and photographs in this book are from my own personal collection, but without access to Michael Luckhurst's excellent collection, this book would not have been possible and I owe him a greater debt of thanks than I could ever repay.

I also wish to thank the following for supplying photographic material: Ciss and Will Akhurst, Eric Moss, Roy and Ivy Glover and Judy Baker. A special vote of thanks to the many photographers whose work appears, including, D. West, W.J. Cox & Sons, Rideouts of Herne Bay and Dennis Print of Scarborough, to mention but a few.

Additional sources of information have come from Bill Austen, Dennis Rodway, Kent County Libraries of Whitstable and Canterbury, Whitstable Museum (Douglas West Collection), *Kentish Gazette* and the newspaper of Adscene Publishing, all of which are greatly appreciated.

I have endeavoured to obtain permission to use material which may still be under copyright and apologise for any omissions in this respect.

The preparation of the manuscript was undertaken by Valerie and Annette Laverick and my daughter Lucy, a thankless task well executed. I am eternally grateful to them.

Introduction

You are invited to travel back in time to visit the heritage town of Whitstable - originally named Witenestaple (White Post) in the 1086 Domesday Survey. My original intention was to celebrate a centenary of this historic town and although I have largely kept to this theme, some inclusions, such as the year 1869, are of special historical interest and could not be left out.

As a native of Whitstable in contact with some of its inhabitants, I have been lucky enough to have acquired some previously unpublished material, some of which is very rare, which has been juxtaposed with more common views. As well as very familiar roads and locations, less familiar images of side roads have been included, which I hope will be of particular interest to past and present residents.

The chapters are divided into six periods of time, each one endeavouring to capture the ever-changing lives of its people, their manner of dress, shops, businesses and modes of transport. The first section features the pre-twentieth century, although the shortage of material produced at this time limits the range of pictures available during the latter part of the nineteenth century.

The early years of the twentieth century are covered in section two, which, because of the abundant material available, shows a broader picture of life in the town and its outskirts. Poor conditions and poverty were widespread, but the resilient Whitstable people tried to make the best of things. The oyster industry, for which the town is famous, is represented, with the rail link and shipping that helped with exports and the local economy. The third section leads up to the thirties, local shops and familiar landmarks are pictured, together with entertainment venues and the arrival of the motor car.

During the 1930s and 1940s featured in the fourth section, much change was to take place. The frozen seas of the '40s and of course, the destruction caused by the horrors of war, are depicted. The towns of Borken in Germany and Dainville in France were linked after the war with Whitstable and appear on the town's main signpost. On the entertainment side, the cinema and theatre had become increasingly popular, along with locally organized events.

The fifth section illustrates the 1950s and the swinging '60s with their changes in fashion, the town having prospered since the early post war years. Photographs of the well documented flood of 1953 and frozen sea of 1963 are included, as well as shops and businesses and the sad removal of the 'World's Oldest Bridge'.

Bringing the history of Whitstable up to date is section six. We see the hustle and bustle of everyday life in a busy thriving town. Architecturally the transformation to a more modern town is slow to happen (many will say thankfully) and a feeling of nostalgia is kept alive.

The final chapter, with its funny postcards, takes a humourous look at Whitstable. Some of these pictures are quite rare and I am pleased to be able to share them with you. Future changes to Whitstable will be greeted with mixed feelings, no doubt, but hopefully they too will be recorded and cherished later by all those who care about this loveable old town.

Real Natives of Whitstable.

One
Late Nineteenth Century

The first few pictures show the storm and flood of 29 November 1897, the first local flood to be recorded by photographs. Their quality reflects their age. This is Nelson Road from Island Wall, the height of the flood being most noticeable in the far right background. The young fireman on the left sports a bowler hat and there is not a wellington boot in sight.

The Salts from Island Wall. The house on the right in Nelson Road and Long Wall, in the left background, is in front of Coastguard Houses in Marine Terrace.

Another view of The Salts looking towards Island Wall with a few houses dotted about. In 1909 this area became the site of Whitstable and Seasalter Golf Club (see p. 12). The building of Middle Wall, Island Wall and Sea Wall prevented the sea from reaching the High Street - unlike 100 years earlier.

Looking down Nelson Road from Westcliff. The high water level clearly shows on the right; it reached the top of the wall and railings of houses Nos 1-9. The construction on the far left is now a dental surgery.

View from Island Wall in the direction of the town. Some fencing is still standing despite a good beating. These buildings are Nos 65 (left) and 67 (right) which stand back some 100 feet from the road. The other houses, such as No. 63 in the far left corner, are nearer the pavement. A young Daniel Sherrin, the popular landscape artist, lived in No. 67 and had No. 65 built for his sister (or so the story goes); he later moved to Joy Lane. No. 65 is probably now over 200 years old.

West Cliff Road on the right, leading to Oxford Street, missed the flood, unlike the lower area on the left (now a golf course, see p. 10).

These houses from No. 12, the Boathouse (left), to No. 5, with the interesting names of Spring Cottage, Seaside Cottage and Neptune Cottage all suffered in the flood. The house with the porch is No 7. Men are wheel-barrowing silt, deposited by the flood, from people's homes. Timber sheds are seen damaged in the background, the house on the left of sterner construction looks relatively unaffected. The left hand house in the row on the right became the office of the Seasalter and Ham Fishery Co. However the Old Neptune Inn, originally a boat building workshop behind the house on the left, was destroyed.

The next six views show Whitstable after the flood. Here is The Cross, with Sea Street going left and Harbour Street to the right. This rare early view of The Duke of Cumberland Hotel shows two dormer windows at the top. A middle one had been added by the turn of the century, necessitating the raising of the sign. This magnificent building was constructed after the Great Fire of 8 October 1866 destroyed the original inn. The Bear and Key public house on the right was established in 1703. Note the man moving sand bags with a hand cart.

The weather-boarded Steam Packet Inn (left) was built in the early nineteenth century next door to and alongside the Harbour Masters' Office and living accommodation. The area directly opposite, by the brick pillar, was later to become Cromwell Road. The shop on the right, No. 97, advertises Hovis Bread. Note the horse and cart taking up over half the width of the road. The pavement on the right would be developed later as buildings were erected. Tankerton Road and Northwood Road are on the horizon and Tower Parade is in the middle rear of the picture.

Whitstable Harbour, with all manner of shipping visible. The houses to the right are in Tower Road.

Whitstable Bay, viewed here from the Horsebridge, was a popular play area for children being only a short walk from the town. Shipping was abundant in these earlier days.

Tankerton Beach, with a path on the left leading to the slopes. The lady holding her hat illustrates the severity of the wind blowing off the sea; has the man on her left lost his?

A view looking the other way down Tankerton Beach. Notice the many ships' masts in the harbour. It took more than bad weather to keep folk off the beach in those days.

Frozen Sea at Whitstable, February, 1895.

The frozen sea off Whitstable Harbour, photographed here in February 1895. The extremely bad weather the 1890s caused great poverty. This picture postcard was produced by W.J. Cox, Whitstable, established in 1863.

Whitstable - Ruins of the Great Fire, November 9th, 1869.

This well known picture, 'Whitstable - Ruins of the Great Fire', 9 November 1869, was produced as a postcard by W.J. Cox in the mid 1900s, showing what was left after a store fire on The Wall. Some twenty-five adjoining houses and fifty-eight storehouses and workshops were burnt down.

Two

Early Twentieth Century

Whitstable—View from Borstal Hill.
1920.

A peaceful view looking down Borstal Hill in 1907. On the far left is the Four Horseshoes public house, built in 1828. The lad in the field is waiting patiently for the next horse-drawn cart to come round the bend! This is the road the traveller would have used for Canterbury some six miles to the north.

A closer look at the Four Horseshoes in 1911. Its landlord then was Mr James Hopkins, who would have welcomed local customers and many cyclists. This was a Fremlins house that later became Shepherd Neame. The lack of motor traffic is highlighted by the angle at which the car is parked, with no pathway on the opposite side.

A most unusual view of the old windmill situated at the top of Borstal Hill. Built in the late eighteenth century, the Borstal Hill Mill was purchased in 1906 by Sir Henry Irving the actor. The man pictured is unknown, but the sign to his right is most clear: 'Private, Trespasses will be prosecuted'.

Gentler times are shown in this 1904 view looking up the hill. The boy poses against the fence leading into grazing fields. The woman and pram in the road are clearly not expecting to meet any fast traffic. There were two other mills in Whitstable at this time: Martindowns off Martindowns Road and Feakins in Belmont Road.

This 1905 scene shows the approach to Borstal Hill with the road bearing to the right. The grey stone building aptly named Stone Cottage, at No. 74, is virtually unchanged today. There are no pavements yet and the road is yet to be resurfaced to take the impending motor traffic.

A far from striking view maybe, but it is included to show a thatched cottage, with the entrance to Borstal Hill Farm and Stables. Manure on the road indicates the path taken by horses to graze in the fields opposite. The pavements were necessitated by the rise in horse-drawn traffic, c. 1911.

A popular postcard view titled Cross Road. After the bottom of the hill the road forks left to Joy Lane and right to the town. The bungalow in the centre of the picture is No. 2 Tollgate House. The tollgate, originally situated at the bottom of Canterbury Road for travellers from Canterbury to the Horsebridge in Whitstable, was moved to make way for the railway bridge built in 1860. The horse trough and pump to the right were donated by Arthur and Myra Pinero in 1896, he being a famous dramatist and playwright. The trough was replaced in 1936 by the Metropolitan Drinking Fountain and Cattle Trough Association.

Joy Lane, c. 1915, looking towards the town and away from Seasalter. The mounds of earth in the view suggest that a pathway would soon be introduced.

An atmospheric picture of life in the fast lane; a 1905 view of Canterbury Road going away from the town, heading towards the hill. Tradesman were a very common sight transporting their wares by horse and cart. The road apparently narrows towards the corner but this is an illusion. The pavement on the right has yet to be completed.

Canterbury Road, c. 1905, and there is no shortage of folk here to say 'cheese' to the photographer. The house on the far left with the chimney stack is No. 90, next to a side road which would later lead to a railway line crossing. Just out of the picture to the left and set back, is The Two Brewers, a public house since 1723. The white walled house to the right is No. 109.

A superb view along Canterbury Road looking east towards the town. The Two Brewers inn (far left) was built originally as a cottage c. 1671. On the near right was the blacksmiths shop and to the side, Forge Lane leading to Saddleton Road. You will notice the pavement starts afterwards and is not very constant on either side of the road. The access gate (furthest left) leads to the railway line. There is an advertisement on the wall to the right for the local *Weekly Times Echo*, priced 1d, and the *Daily Chronicle*. The Noahs Ark public house is the building on the right after the trees.

An unusual view of Canterbury Road from the railway bridge in Oxford Street. Rollington's Haircutting Saloon is on the left at No. 17 with its long barber's pole. Next door is a private house later to become Sunshine Stores; next left is Carter's butchers, later to become Tattersalls. A lady and gent walk their bicycles along the road, a common form of transport at this time.

An early twentieth-century look at Saddleton Road, away from the town. At No. 2 is E. Foreman, a bakers shop, the only shop premises in the road. For the benefit of present residents of the other houses in the picture, they are, from left to right: Nos 6b, 8, 10 and 12 followed by the detached houses, Nos 14 and 16. The sole house on the right is 11a (now known as Brenda House) which was built around this time; other buildings would soon follow (see p. 101).

Oxford Street, 1906, viewed from the railway bridge heading towards the town. The confectioners and tobacconists of J. Birch (far left) display interesting signs showing W.D. & H.O. Wills Gold Flake tobacco at 10 ounces for 3s and Cadbury's Chocolate for sale. Further down the road on the left is The East Kent Tavern, indicated by a white sign partially obscured by trees; the landlord's name was Mr Gurr. The inn was established in 1860 and continues to run successfully today. On the right is Howe's grocers.

Oxford Street again but in 1912; J. Birch has become W. Hales, but is still in the same line of business with added signs for Taddy's Imperial Tobacco and Idris Soda Water. A bakers shop on the far right advertises Turog Bread. Beyond the second horse and cart is Cromwell Road (to the right) and Clifton Road (opposite).

24

The railway bridge in this picture is partially obscured. The bridge was built in 1860 to enable the railway line to be extended to Thanet. To the left of the bridge over the road joining Oxford Street with Canterbury Road, Whitstable railway station was built. The station moved to its existing location in Old Bridge Road in 1914. On the left the dormer-windowed private house of No. 61 became a dental surgery in the '50s and '60s and is now The British Legion Social Centre. The Railway Inn (facing) at 1 Canterbury Road first opened as a beerhouse in 1845. It prospered with its regular railway visitors, but closed in the mid 1970s and is now a private house.

Jackson's grocers and Post Office Stores at 59 Canterbury Road, on the corner with Harwich Street. Mrs Jackson and her daughter are posing for the camera. The sign below the post box indicates Edward VII's reign, suggesting that the photograph dates from some time between between 1901 and 1910. Christmas cards advertised (left) tell us that the picture was probably taken late in the year. The gas lamp and telephone sign, together with so many goods advertised, make this a very informative view. The business was to continue for many years.

High Street, *c.* 1900. The Ship Inn (far right; brewers Ash & Co.) had as its landlord Bill Gammon, an ex-marine and Whitstable Town Crier (at 1s 6d a time). Built in 1750 it was later renamed The Ship Centurion and modernised in 1914. The light coloured building further down the road with the first canopy was the Queens Head. Immediately before that, set back, is St Alphege Church. A copy of this picture has pride of place inside the pub today.

High Street, *c.* 1905. The Queens Head (far right) was established in 1845. The brewers were Flint & Co. from Canterbury, but a decline in trade forced its closure in 1912. It is now a book shop. Nearest left is Pullar's Dye Works at Nos 100 and 102. Approaching the end of the road to the right is Gladstone Road. Shops were intermingled with private houses.

Looking up the town, c. 1910. The Queens Head Inn is in the distance. The building with a wall jutting out on the right was R.E. Uden, estate agent; next door at No. 56 was O. Holden, grocers. In the nearest building, Nos 48-54, were Church and Co., furniture dealers, whose premises later became The Picture House cinema; next was a drapers shop, E. Jackson, tailor and a tobacconists. The shops to the left remain unidentified.

In 1904, further up the town, at No. 24 was F.G. Richards, fruiterer; at No.26 Ainsley Bros butchers, proprietor H. Hadler; Nos 28 and 30 were the Royal Naval Reserve public house. Next door at No. 32 was Freeman Hardy and Willis' shoe shop and at No. 34 was E. Wastall, wine merchants, which became Woolworths in 1933. The road does not seem to be in very good condition.

A piece of Whitstable's history, c. 1895. Identification is not easy, but thanks to Whitstable Museum, some details are known. Far right, Wheelers Oyster Rooms were established in 1856 at No. 8; No. 10 was the London Studio (photography); No. 12 a hairdressers; No. 14 was the General Furnishing Warehouse, established 1854. Further along the road, just after the Royal Naval Reserve Public House at No. 32 was Gurston Commercial Hotel and Dining Rooms, later to become Freeman Hardy and Willis. On the left the shops were known as 'Cheapside'; Harrison and Co., ironmongers and general decorators were at No. 35. Public houses called Holy Endeavour (1845-1906) at No. 21; The Shades (1878-1906) at No. 19 and The Prince of Wales (1863-1967) just out of picture at No.13, were in close proximity to five other drinking houses not pictured. H. Hemley's Supply Stores barrow can be identified in the road on the left.

The Duke of Cumberland, now with three gabled windows, 1905. Furthest left is the shoe shop, Freeman Hardy and Willis (now only at Herne Bay and Hythe), then the Royal Naval Reserve (brewers Rigdens Ales and Stouts). At No. 9 near the Bear and Key hotel was T. Staniland, outfitters. The Prince of Wales public house was two doors further up the street.

A view of the Australian Emigration Agency, 1911, to the left, between No. 24 Mrs Truscott's restaurant and the recently opened Ainslay Bros butchers at No. 26. The *Whitstable Times* office at 37 High Street, just out of the picture right, (later Cox's Publishers) reported 'Free and Assisted Passages, farm workers and servant girls required with much more assistance on arrival'. The first steam ship to Australia left the harbour in 1837. The Prince of Wales public house (far right) used the brewers Flint & Co. Checksfields the tobacconist was at No. 11 for many years; S.T. Hatchards outfitters was at No. 9 and Solley, china dealers, occupied No. 7, next door to the Bear and Key hotel.

A similar view from 1900 to that on the previous page, but here showing some of the ever-changing businesses in the town. The butchers at No. 38 was called H.C. Wilkes; next door was Sayers & Small, drapers and at No. 34, E. Wastall's wine merchants. The building on the right, with the dark gas lamp outside and protruding pole was Whitstable Fire Station until the late 1920s. Alfred Gann was the captain. A corn merchants was based at No. 23, probably owned by Mr G. Denne.

A final look at the bottom of the town in 1914. Wheelers Oyster Co., pictured in many views and a focal point for visitors, is seen on the far left, Note the banner on the left before Sea Street advertising *The Mermaid Empress*, sailing to Ireland on Monday 2 July.

View from Ludgate Hill into Harbour Street to the left and Sea Street to the right, 1908. The central building was erected in about 1905 by Fred Goldfinch and rented by Wallace Pring, a reportedly eccentric dressmaker, in 1912. In 1865 The Railway Tavern (just out of picture to the left) was renamed The Punch Tavern. The man with a hand cart illustrates that no one-way system was yet in place! The walkway on the far right is known as Sea Wall.

Harbour Street, Whitstable

A 1912 view into Harbour Street. The Lipton Tea House (far left) at No. 31, was a seventeenth-century building with a sweet shop (doorway far left) and a famous low-ceilinged entrance. The shop closed in 1982. The Tudor Tea Rooms, established next door were visited by one of Whitstable's most famous residents, the late Peter Cushing. The building to the far right opened as the Palais de Luxe cinema in 1913 but closed in 1931. Pollard's gents outfitters were at No. 26 and at No. 25 was W.H. Retter, drapers. The motor repairs and garage sign posted (left) referred to premises on the other side of the road, at No. 45, called Foads.

A rare glimpse of Clifton Road (incorrectly named Westcliff Road on the postcard), *c.* 1908. The sign of A.E. Cooke, practical tailor, hangs outside No. 3. The first row of houses was known as Clifton Terrace. On the left side old houses have largely been replaced with more modern ones.

Looking towards West Cliff from grasslands, divided by a lovely stream. This area was flooded in 1897. Just beyond the houses on the left is Nelson Road leading back to the town.

Wave Crest, along the beach from the Neptune public house, 1910. The beached schooner *Vigilant*, (right) has been used in recent years by the Whitstable Sea Scouts as a training ship. Portable changing chalets down on the beach were used by holidaymakers staying in the row of houses above. The majority of holidaymakers were Londoners.

This undated postcard depicts The Slip at Wave Crest. Locals would dig here for seafood such as cockles, winkles and whelks. The boat house (right) attended to ship repairs, such as the one in dock.

This postcard, 'A Glimpse of Whitstable' by Rideouts, looks onto Reeves Beach (named after Josiah Reeves, a nearby timber yard owner). This walkway, called the Sea Wall separates the Horsebridge at the end of the High Street and Ludgate Hill, at the end of Harbour Street. The house with the white wall is called The Cottage. Notice the goods train nearing the end of the track.

A postcard view from the Whitstable end of Tankerton beach in September 1907, 'Whitstable Bay and Pier Head' by W.J. Cox.

A sad reminder that many whales have been stranded during low tide at Whitstable Harbour. This one was 10 ft long and quite a curiosity. The child entrepreneur would try to sell 'a look' for 2d to the public. This audience posed on 23 November 1905.

Whitstable oyster dredging boats at work in 1907. They usually carried a four man crew and towed rowing boats behind. The three sails were called the top sail, main sail and fore sail. Over 100 dredgers were in operation at Whitstable in 1900.

Once caught, the oysters were landed from rowing boats. The fishermen wore Guernsey jumpers, Cheese Cutter caps and knee length boots. They needed strong arms and shoulders for this job and there was always plenty of employment available as this was the town's prime industry. These grim faced fishermen were pleased to pose for the photographer in 1915.

Oarsman and oyster sack carriers were asked to pose for the camera. Some of the oyster fleet can be seen on the horizon. The shipping industry kept local unemployment to a minimum. Note at the bottom right hand corner, the seal of the Corporation of Dredgers of Whitstable of 1793.

This rare view shows the oystermen loading the oyster sacks from the boats at Whitstable harbour to a waiting horse and cart, *c.* 1910. The bags were despatched to two main companies, Whitstable Oyster Fishery Co. and Seasalter and Ham Oyster Co. at the Horsebridge and East Quay.

Fisher girls hard at work, shortly before the First World War. It was their job to sort, grade and pack oysters, ready for dispatch to other parts of the world. The girls' headscarves show how cold it must have been. The foreman, complete with pipe, does the paper work. Millions of oysters were caught every year, but a decline was starting by 1920 through neglect during the war and problems of frost, disease and pollution which were killing off the 'native' oyster.

This next selection of postcards shows once again the ever-changing ownership of shops. In this 1905 view of Tankerton Terrace, No. 1 is San Toy Tea Rooms; No. 2 Tankerton Post Office; next door Home and General Accounts. The old man in the road with spade in hand had a most enviable job! The entrance to Tankerton Towers can be seen on the left.

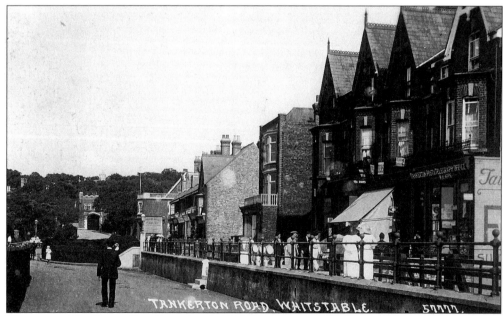

This view, 'Tankerton Road', is dated 1915. Tankerton Post and Telegraph Office (W.H. Apps) has taken over the San Toy Tea Rooms. Wells & Evans' fancy repository store is at No. 2 and has attracted a large crowd. This early warehouse used the shop frontage to full advantage; Smith the baker can be seen facing at the end.

The Postmaster General issued an instruction for messages on postcards to cover at least one third of the picture side, with the name and address on the reverse. This one, dated 1902, was one of the last ones to be produced. Luckily, given the untidy format, they were soon to be discontinued.

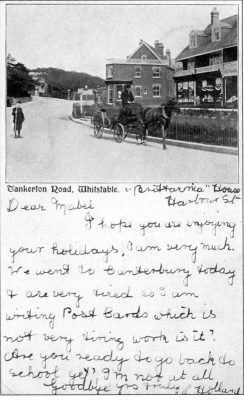

Tankerton Road, Whitstable.

Dear Mabel
I hope you are enjoying your holidays, I am very much. We went to Canterbury today & are very tired so I am writing Post Cards which is not very tiring work is it? Are you ready to go back to school yet? I'm not at all Goodbye

The year is now 1902. J. Lawson, estate agent is at No. 5 on the right and Hall's Refreshment Rooms are at No. 4. Tankerton Estate Office, here until the mid 1920s, was responsible for the construction of Tankerton Road. Mrs Goldfinch owned the building, far right, which later opened as a greengrocers.

By 1906 Tankerton Road had become Tower Parade. From left to right: C. Coleman, Miss M. Prior, Tankerton Estate Office, Mrs G.N.J. Buckstone, ladies outfitters, Daniels and Collar, fancy repository (also at Nos 100 and 102 High Street until 1937) and Mrs Goldfinch, greengrocer.

Tower Parade, 1911. This interesting head-on view shows Queen Victoria's Jubilee Memorial Fountain. The fountain was made of green glazed tiles. The long shadows along with one chap shielding his eyes from the sun and another squinting, indicates a hot afternoon in late summer. The shops are closed and blinds pulled down. The shops from left to right are: C. Coleman, a provision store, Miss M. Prior, confectioner, South Tankerton Estate Office and behind a tree, S.E. Kemp, fancy drapers.

Tower Parade from a different perspective, pre-1920. The Tankerton bakery of P. Smith is clearly shown. Mrs M. Child, greengrocer, appears furthest right. The Castle, previously called Tankerton Towers, can be seen behind the entrance door in the background. The drinking fountain sports a heavy iron mug and chain and shrubs surround the grassed area.

Tankerton Terrace, c. 1900. A fashion conscious lady in white has just arrived to do some shopping - a major outing in those days. Other people in smart horse-drawn carriages make this a very genteel scene. The road was originally made of granite.

This rare panoramic postcard of Tower Road in the early years of this century shows a view of both sides of the road. The Bijou Tearooms are advertised on the left, along with Triumph and Rudge Whitworth motor cycles. Private houses can now be seen opposite the line of shops.

A view of the signal box, the level crossing (middle) and Whitstable on the other side of the road. This was the Whitstable to Canterbury railway, known affectionately as the 'Crab and Winkle Line'. C. Coleman's stores are on the corner of Tower Parade. Three wheelers were quite popular at this time. Unlike the Parade, pavements had yet to be constructed towards the station, which looks very busy. Northdown Road goes to the left and Beach Walk to the right.

Tower Road, Tankerton.

A glimpse of the railway signal box. It is interesting to see the addition of a single storey building to the shops mentioned earlier. Masts on the right indicate the position of the harbour, and the fishery warehouses, also on the right, have roofs in need of urgent repair.

The Picture House cinema at 48 High Street, previously the furniture store of Church & Co., was rebuilt in 1911 and opened as a cinema in 1913. It was run by Mr Paton, whose wife played piano for the silent films. Entrance was from the side as the screen was immediately behind the front wall; cut out tickets were issued from semi-circular booths at the front. In 1928 the cinema was renamed the Whitstable Electric Theatre Company before reverting back to its original name. It was rebuilt as the Argosy in 1937, severely damaged by the flood of 1953, reopened as the Regal and finally closed in 1960. There were three other cinemas, the Oxford Picture House (until 1984), the Palais De Luxe in Harbour Street and the Trocadero in Marine Parade.

Barn House, Joy Lane, c. 1913. This building was purchased for Queen Mary as a coronation gift and was then donated for use as a holiday home for working girls. It opened on 6 July 1912 and servants were probably sent there by their employers. Built in the fifteenth century it was used during the First World War as a convalescent home for wounded soldiers, reverting to its original purpose afterwards.

A rare chance to see the garden at the back of Barn House from just inside one of the many entrances.

A picture postcard of Queen Mary (arrowed) making a well documented visit to Whitstable on 15 September 1915, accompanied by a lady in waiting (to the right). Arriving at the station on the South Eastern and Central Railway line from London she crossed over the footbridge on the Railway Avenue side to Old Bridge Road on this side and into the waiting open-topped touring Vauxhall motor car, driven by Miss Dot Carson, to visit and inspect Barn House.

The next few pictures show some well known buildings. This one is Tankerton Towers in 1906, which was renamed The Castle. It was built in 1792 as the official residence of the Lord of the Manor of Tankerton. Classed as a small castled manor, it one of Tankerton's best known landmarks.

THE OLD PARSONAGE. WHITSTABLE.

The Old Parsonage, 1907. The date on the front of the house is 1461, making it possibly the oldest surviving house in the area. A farm in the 1860s, it became the residence of the Rector to All Saints Church (right). The pond was later filled in for the playing fields development. I hope the fisherman landed a whopper that day!

Seasalter Parish Church was built in 1844 and was later known as St Alphege Church. We see it here in 1910. This part of Whitstable was included in Seasalter Parish in the nineteenth century. Situated in the High Street alongside No. 99, the railings surrounding the front were removed for Second World War metal salvage. The small building to the right and alongside was a butcher's slaughter house. It is still standing today but is no longer visible from the road.

St Mary's Parish Church, built by G.E. Foad and opened on 25 April 1906, still looks good today. Situated to the right of the Oxford cinema it is now used as a hall for various functions and jumble sales.

This is a 1904 view. The first house along Marine Parade in a row of houses named Cliff Terrace, was built in 1899 by Gann & Co. Its Victorian architectural design was described at the time as 'classy'. London Hospital started a convalescent home here in 1899 which was used during the First World War for casualties. Arthur Fitt purchased the whole property and converted the far right hand side to form the Marine Hotel, later expanding it even further. At the rear towards Tankerton Road his brother George developed the premises into a garage to become George Fitt Motors, a very successful business.

POST OFFICE, SWALECLIFFE. *(Near Whitstable.)*

Swalecliffe Post Office opened in the early 1900s in a converted thatched cottage. Next door but one, at 66 Herne Bay Road, was the Fan public house. Little information is available on this inn other than it is said to have been used as a 'safe house' for French prisoners of war during the Napoleonic era. The old cottage walls were rebuilt with brick in 1913, three years after this photograph was taken.

The junction at Swalecliffe in about 1909. The distance to Whitstable, going left, would have been about 2 miles; to Herne Bay, straight on, about 1 and 1/2 miles and to Canterbury, to the right, about 7 miles. The chap with the horse and cart delivered fresh, homemade bread every day to customers from Whitstable to Herne Bay.

Church Street, 1910. Before Tankerton Estate Agency formed the new road in 1890, Church Street was the only through road to Swalecliffe and Herne Bay from Whitstable. The Monument public house is on the left with the sign near the chimneys. First licensed in 1731 and purchased along with the forge opposite, John Hayward held the longest tenancy, lasting from 1913 to 1936. It is now a Whitbread house. The blacksmith's forge functioned well into the twentieth century. It became Mr Kirby's furniture shop and was then pulled down to make the car park entrance for All Saints Church next door. Church Street leads from the entrance road to the railway station.

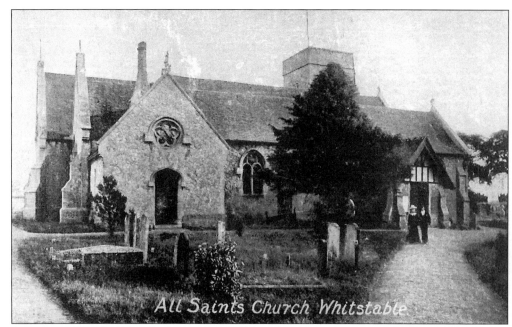

All Saints Church, Church Street, was built in the fifteenth century; a full restoration was undertaken in 1875. The churchyard was closed in 1857 and burials were undertaken at Millstrood Hill, reverting back to All Saints in 1874 following a gift of land by Mr Wynn Ellis.

This view of the harbour, shows just how many vessels it could accommodate, c. 1914. The lighthouse can be seen to the right. Views of the harbour, in postcard form, were very popular with holidaymakers.

The Tankerton Hotel, 1913. The hotel was built in 1902, changing its name to the Tankerton Arms in 1980. The cordoned-off area owned by the brewers was used as an open air concert venue, most famously by the *Jollity Boys*; later a covered stage was erected. Poor demand after the Second World War meant that the upper rooms were converted to flats and the restaurant closed, hence the eventual change of name. The area to the left, called The Shubbery, leads to Tankerton Slopes.

A typical scene in 1905 with plenty of bars, cafes and amusements to attract the holidaymaker. Mrs Anne Kemp's refreshment tea rooms are advertised. Swingboats, all the rage from the 1890s, needed just one lad to collect the fares for a modest wage. They were pulled down in 1953 after the floods of the early '50s. The pebble beach has not deterred this little girl bringing a spade.

Beach Walk in 1909. Adults talk or sit passing the time while children play on the beach. The Royal Cafe is advertised on a house side wall while a cafeteria can be seen on a roof. Everybody seems to be over-dressed by today's standards. The harbour can be seen on the horizon.

The same year but looking away from Beach Walk. Two children play on a boat launcher. Four posts indicate the walkway to Tankerton Slopes while a sign on the edge of the land to the right states 'No admittance Trespassers will be prosecuted'.

Three

Up to the 1930s

Whitstable High St.

This is almost certainly a pre-1920 Congregational Sunday School procession when an annual treat for children was a walk through the town followed by a tea party held in a local field. The procession is led by church dignitaries and teachers. A red herring is the Jubilee flag, partially obscured, which might suggest Queen Victoria's Jubilee in 1887, however, the family butchers of Surmans and the fashions all suggest otherwise.

Looking down the High Street, c. 1920. Furthest left is Scott & Son, cleaners and dyers; next door at No. 66 is E.A. Cooke, tailor. West & Son occupied No. 64, Douglas joining his father Stephen in 1919; in the '20s they expanded to No. 66. At No. 62 Miss A. Watts had a fancy drapers shop. Advertised as The Real Canterbury Lamb Shop, No. 60 was called The London Central Meat Co. Ltd. Opposite is Henry George Surmans' butchers shop, trading for over fifty years, since the early part of this century, as a family business at Nos 59 and 61, then at Nos 57 and 59. No. 61 became the South Eastern Trustee Savings Bank in the 1950s; No. 65, nearest right, was W. Holden, watchmaker and repairs, sandwiched in between was No. 63 a bakers shop; No. 57 at this time was J. Hamilton, upholsterers.

Mr Maynard, Manager of the London Central Meat Co. Ltd, c. 1924. The firm traded here from the early 1900s until 1938. It is now a clothes shop.

This picture, c. 1920, shows Nos 103 and 105 High Street under the name of M. Barnes, fancy draper. H. Wilmans, furnishers, at Nos 107 and 109, from around 1915-1934, was to be taken over by Ryes in 1935. The Ship Centurion public house stood next door. Wilmans was one of the first shops to be lit by electricity.

Looking down the town towards the Duke of Cumberland Hotel in the 1920s. Far left at Nos 78, 80 and 82 High Street is L.J. Foreman, tailors; the size of their premises suggests a flourishing business. Hardings the hairdresser was at No. 76, and the spire shows the site of the Salvation Army Hall at No. 74. Opposite, on the right, stands Jessie Webbs, newsagents, which traded from the early 1920s until the '80s.

The Salvation Army Hall (left). We are unable to confirm the identity of the hair cutting and shaving saloon at No. 73, with four barbers shops spanning the time from the turn of the century until the 1940s. C.J. Roses, watchmakers, at No. 79 also traded for a long time. The group of people on the pavement to the left are outside No. 70 which later became the General Post Office.

A view of the reservoir at the Gorrell Tank. Station Road goes to the left with Cromwell Road along the back of the picture. The Millstrood and Gorrell streams run into the reservoir. In 1970 it was concreted over and is now used as a general car park, which is at its busiest on Thursdays - market day (see p. 122).

Joy Lane, *c.* 1920, with an open tourer cruising happily along. No congestion to worry about, just the fear of mechanical failure - common in the early days of the motor car. Notice the pavement made up on the left side with the right hand side about to be attended to!

Westcliff Road, just off Nelson Road, *c.* 1926. The car, a Humber probably, signals that the age of the motor car has dawned and the days of horse-drawn traffic are numbered.

Pageants were very popular in the 1920s and '30s. these lads pose happily as Red Indians, probably to take part in a carnival parade, where they would compete for prizes.

This delightful scene shows young ladies practising for Whitstable Carnival in a back garden, c 1922. Their ages seem to determine their position in the formation dance sequence.

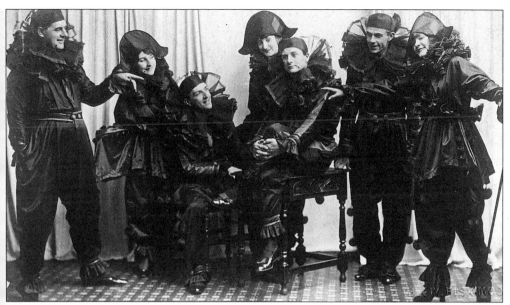

Popular entertainers the *Lead Swingers*, c. 1920. They would play at venues such as the Palais de Luxe cinema and concert hall in Harbour Street which opened just before the First World War.

A concert party production of Randell Jackson's *1929 Bohemians*, a play performed at the lawn pavilion, Tankerton. Groups like the *Jollity Boys* would perform there and in outdoor arenas such as that opposite the Tankerton Hotel on the Slopes, now a well known picnic area. Such theatrical shows were very popular up and down the country in the '20s and '30s.

The Lady Chapel inside All Saints Parish Church.

Inside Whitstable Church, looking towards the main altar, c. 1920. The three stained glass windows show biblical figures to stunning effect.

Queen Marys Convalescent Home,
Whitstable.

A bright summer day in 1926 shows Queen Mary's Convalescent Home in Joy Lane, at this time used mainly as a holiday and convalescent home for the under privileged.

The Oval skating rink, opened in 1914 (but only for a few years) and was situated by the Sea Wall. Music was supplied by an electric organ and a restaurant to the right of the view served teas and light refreshments, with changing rooms down below. Fancy dress carnival competitions were held there and there were fairy lights around the perimeter. Children could skate for 6d an hour or 1s 6d if skates were borrowed. Notice the oyster fleet on the horizon.

Marine Terrace, 1918. The Neptune public house, in the distance, was rebuilt after the 1897 flood using material from two cottages on the west side of the old site. It stands on the beach, enduring the ravages of all weather conditions. More houses have been added here since 1897. The people's clothes and the canopied deck chair imply a fine summer day. Island Wall is situated behind the row of houses.

Moving to 1926, this view of the terrace, now called Marine Parade, shows the emergence of a shallow sea wall in the forefront, with the pathway ending just after the two bollards. The young children seem only too pleased to be able to play a part in the picture.

The Old Forge converted into a tobacconists and general store, with the old post office to the right. This 1912 view shows the old cottage shortly before the walls were bricked.

The *Vigilant* in shallow water, 1922. The terraced houses on the right were very popular as holiday homes, there were changing chalets on the beach. Whitstable at this time was one of the most popular seaside resorts for Londoners. The Old Neptune public house is in the distance.

The year is now 1925 and the London Convalescent Home has become The Marine Hotel, the telephone number for which was Whitstable 72. The postage for a postcard had increased from one halfpenny to one penny.

The Coastguards along Seasalter sea front, 1925. Unlike the shelter on West Beach this is just a cordoned-off area with wooden fencing characteristic of the area.

An informative picture brim-full of nostalgia. The building on the left with the white roof is the Seasalter and Ham Oyster Fishery Stores; fish boxes are stacked outside. Although called the Lighthouse, the tall lean structure is actually a last relic of the 'Crab and Winkle' railway from the Canterbury and Whitstable line. It is a chimney alongside the old engine house. A stationary steam engine was used in the early 1830s to haul the heavy locomotives and wagons up hill by rope, the loco having little power. There were three other engines on the route. The area is now a car park. Extensive work was carried out on the East Quay which reopened in 1963.

This sketch depicts the opening of the Canterbury and Whitstable Railway on 3 May 1830, the first in the world to introduce a steam hauled passenger service. The journey was some 6 miles; 4 miles using stationary steam winding engines and 2 miles by locomotive power alone in the early years. Its most famous and original engine, *Invicta*, lasted about a year and was displayed in Canterbury well into the 1970s, before full restoration in 1979.

A bird's eye view showing the ceremony of the unveiling of the War Memorial, draped in a Union Jack, on 1 April 1920. The iron railing enclosure has long since gone, as has the tall flag pole. The premises to the left were the old Council Offices and are now the library. The Coach and Horses public house (built 1830) is on the far right.

A closer look at the War Memorial in Oxford Street. The column is made of granite set on a square base. Some 178 names are honoured from the First World War with the dead of the Second World War remembered on a scroll. At the top of the column is a cross resting on a lamp. Annual remembrances have been held since the year of its unveiling.

S. 5460. Harbour Street, Whitstable.

Harbour Street, *c.* 1917. At No. 39 is Coleman's Post Office and Stores; on the corner to the right is F.A. Boulders; shipping supplies can be seen advertised. Foad Motor repairs and garage is signposted as being on the other side of the road, at No. 45, which was owned and rented out by Mr Davey, the solicitor. Before becoming involved with motor vehicles this was a cycle shop and after 1935 became a cycle shop once again. J. Saunders was at No. 48(facing) and is now the Chatterbox Coffee House. Two young girls can be seen entering Mr Weston's sweet shop at No. 31, beside the Lipton Tea House.

Looking from Harbour Street towards the town, *c.* 1925. On the right side of the road, well illustrated on the side wall, is Cycle Radio, dealing in both wireless and bicycles. There is a chemists next door which still trades as a pharmacy today. To the left at No. 45 is Foads Garage; the rear entrance was in Albert Street, just out of the picture further left. Davey's outfitters was on the corner, the Davey's being the family renting out No. 45. The barbers is signposted 'Gents Saloon' with a striped barbers pole.

Lower Parade in the 1920s. The road going to the left leads to Tower Parade. There are tea rooms in abundance along the sea front including Angels, Butlers and Kemps.

Tankerton Beach, looking towards Lower Parade in the distance, with the ever popular swing boats. How nice to see a smiling face as the young lady, with poodle in tow, happily poses for the camera.

Further along the shore line off Tankerton Slopes is this busy scene on the beach, sometime before 1920. It's amazing to see the number of people the sea front attracted on a hot summer day. There is plenty of activity in the sea with rowing boats for hire and sailing boats in evidence.

Back to Tower Parade with a close-up view of Queen Victoria's Jubilee Fountain and The Castle entrance, far right, with the road bending left towards Tankerton. Shrubs form the boundary of this most unusual piece of ground.

Tower Parade with Tankerton bakery on the corner, 1920s. On the opposite side of the road is E.R. Haslett's high class grocery stores at No. 1. At No. 2 is J.H. Reeves, dairy, and Tankerton Estate Office can still be seen. On the right is W.H. Dadd selling sports shoes and fancy goods as well as offering boot repairs. He also had a bazaar on the opposite side of the road, down Beach Road. In the 1930s, to the left of the fancy goods shop, where the bowling alley now stands, there used to be a circus. However, lack of interest caused an early closure. Dempster's refreshment bar can be seen adjoining to the left. This area, well known for its amusement arcades, drew holidaymakers like a magnet. The buildings on the right were shortly to be demolished.

In the harbour a variety of marine craft can be seen moored c. 1927. Unlike the roads, the harbour was very busy with traffic, from rowing boats and sailing boats for pleasure to the larger oyster boats for business.

This chilling view sums up the feelings of these two fisherman with their beached schooner on the frozen sea of 15 February 1929. There was no fear of the ice breaking and them falling in.

Another view of the frozen sea. The thickness of the ice out to sea can be judged by the number of boats lying on top of it. The main factor causing the freeze was the volume of river water entering the sea at the estuaries of the Medway, fresh water freezing at a higher temperature than salt. There were similar occurrences in 1938, 1940, 1947, 1956, 1958 and 1963, but winters have not been cold enough for it to have happened in more recent years.

The Oxford Picture Hall entrance, *c.* 1922. The film showing was *Out of the Depths*, the programme billed in two parts: *The Reward* and *Scotland For Ever*. The first film was shown here in 1912, the building was demolished in 1935. The new cinema, on the same site, showed films until 1984.

Four
The 1930s and '40s

The Picture House cinema has now become the Argosy, opened early in 1937. Here the building is illuminated and has a crown to celebrate the coronation of King George VI later that year. On the board outside we have a glimpse of the films being shown around this time: *Land Lover* with Jack Melford; Clive Brooks and Tutta Ralf in *Dressed to Kill*, Randolph Scott in *Last of the Mohicans* and lastly *Bottle Party*. Admission ranged from 6d in the stalls to 1s 6d in the circle and half price for children. Pictures like this were given to cinema employees as a souvenir. This cinema was later renamed The Regal.

Looking down the High Street, 1934. Woolworth's (left), at Nos 34 and 36 was known at its opening in 1933 as the 'sixpenny bazaar' as all items were this price or cheaper. At 36a (far left) was J. Newell & Co. drapers. Further down the road beyond the Royal Naval Reserve public house was E. Wastell, wine merchants, who had previously, with Newells, occupied the Woolworth's site. Dewhurst the butchers, later to become Stewarts, is next door with the canopy at No. 26. The Home and Colonial Stores (far right) is at No. 29 after moving in the early '30s from No. 19. W.H. Huxtable, confectioners is next door. The old fire brigade station at No. 25 has been replaced by Thomas Rigdon, corn merchants and at No. 17 is Arthur Collar's, general merchants, selling lavatories, stoves and baths; their main premises were further up the road at No. 35.

A few years later the sign has changed on the Home and Colonial Stores and Arthur Collar's Ltd now inhabit Nos 33 and 35. At No. 31 is H. Couchman, fruiterers, with their trade bicycle outside. Cycling was very popular and no car parking restrictions were necessary at this time.

Canterbury Road looking towards Oxford Street, c. 1930. On the far right is Noah's Ark public house, the selling of beer from these premises dates back to the 1850s. With new housing developments in the '60s and '70s trade improved and this is a very popular ale house today. Its present licensee, Mr Dennis Rodway took over from a 95 year old landlord on 6 November 1963. This area is dominated by residential housing. Suffolk Street and Norfolk Street lead off to the left and Harwich Street is further down to the right. Previously on the left, by the sign, was a milestone indicating London, 65 miles.

This postcard scene has been identified as Day's Garage at No. 6 Oxford Street in the 1930s. The building dates from 1889. There was no forecourt at the pumps so petrol was pumped to parked cars in the road by an overhead extending cable, at 1s 5d a gallon. The petrol pump attendent shyly hides behind the pump while the two boys pose on their scooters. Note the one front brake lever. Mr Ron Smith took over the garage in the 1950s but little information has come to light about Mr Day, the original owner.

Two carnival floats in Cromwell Road. With a huge crowd watching along the route that went through the town, this was a good opportunity to advertise. On this occasion we see the Pram Shop in Oxford Street advertised and a big baby in the pram promoting Read's Dairy. The carnival was at its most popular from the 1920s to the 1950s.

A Whitstable Carnival float by the Whitstable Cycling Club, c. 1939. Standing, left, is Mr Revell alongside George Coleman. The lad on top with the pipe is Ken Moss. They have either won a cup in the carnival or maybe a race with other clubs earlier! Many cycling outings and races were organized by the club which was established in 1935 at West Beach. They moved to premises behind Webb's paper shop in the High Street and finally to a building later to become Barton's boat shop. Reduced attendance due to the war brought the club to an end in the 1940s.

An unusual scene photographed by West & Son in 1935 outside the Duke of Cumberland Hotel following the promotional visit to the town by four eastern ladies, known at the local visiting circus as the Giraffe Neck Women. To the left is Sergeant Rivers, a familiar and popular policeman at the time, keeping an eye on the proceedings.

This group of people are awaiting the return, of children, from an outing. This 1930s scene typifies the dress of the period; hats were worn all year round.

The next four pictures by West & Son capture the times superbly. In August 1939, just prior to the outbreak of war, the roads were awash. This view of the High Street shows Boots the Chemist, the post office and Scott's Cleaners. The motorcycle and car have been abandoned but one brave driver tries to get through.

On the other side of the road can be seen Barclays Bank. After Gladstone Road and on the corner is Smith Brothers, bakers, at No. 69. Just behind the bus, the building with the shaving sign, is W. George & Son, hairdressers at No. 73. To complete the identification, No. 75 was S. Perky Stores with G. King the bakers at No. 77 under the Vitbe sign. The High Street was just passable to most traffic, after some 5 inches of rain, but not for these abandoned bicycles.

The frozen sea of 18 January 1940. With the war only a few months old pictures that were taken at the time were withdrawn from publication for defence reasons.

Another freeze, this time on 24 February 1947. The awesome effect of the cold can be seen and much harm was done to sea life and the fishing industry.

A view taken by West's looking up Ludgate Hill towards the harbour entrance in 1940. The low grey building on the left was stabling for railway horses. The row of houses on the right, known as 'Starvation Point', lies derelict but in their hey-day included the South Eastern Railway Tavern, a public house from 1863-1927 and later a private house. The row had also contained an amusement arcade at the far end, (round the corner) and small cafes, one of which was owned, in 1946, by the author's father as an ice cream shop, at No. 79 Harbour Street. Demolition took place in the early '60s. Notice the Dilnot's van owned by Mr Dilnot the baker, who occupied a shop in Oxford Street before moving to 77 High Street.

A local meeting between Whitstable Council and delegates and members of Whitstable Bowling Club with their familiar trilby hats; Mr Speaker is addressing the assembly. The president and vice-president can be seen seated, their chains of office visible, alongside various councillors. The minutes of the meeting are recorded by the chap in the front row, third from the right. This was photographed, in the 1940s, in The Castle grounds in Tankerton, near to the bowling green. Notice the two first aid attendants at the back.

The Hotel Continental along Beach Road at Tankerton, in 1933, was originally a weather-boarded construction but, around 1890, it was redesigned and rebuilt of brick. Mr Vittore Offredi took over the running of it in the 1920s. The family firm of Offredi & Son also ran a restaurant at 29 High Street for about a decade until the early 1920s. Next door was a boarding house called Beulah, which became the Three Castles Restaurant. Later the two buildings merged to become the Continental with the right side becoming the bar. Today called the Harbour Lights, it has been converted into flats but still has a bar to the right.

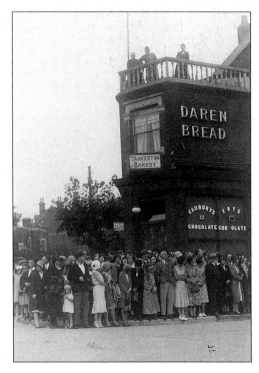

Tankerton Bakery, 2-4 Tankerton Road, alongside Northwood Road, c. 1940. The people are probably awaiting the carnival procession from their left. Fashions have become noticeably less formal.

The after effect of a lorry losing control and hitting Boon's Cafe at the top of Borstal Hill, by the roundabout, in 1938. The filling station, which is just out of the picture, was run by John and Jack Boon and partly owned by Mr F. Thorogood of Northwood Garage in Tankerton. The Thanet Way Road goes off to the right.

This second view shows the vehicle involved and a close up of the damage caused. Curious spectators watch - some things never change!

No chance of getting away with this accident with the company's name and address is well captured on film! A workman evaluates the difficulty of removing the lorry.

Looking inside the cafe we can see the damage caused to the kitchen where the lorry went in. The cafe was run by Mrs Winifred Boon until it changed hands in the mid 1950s. The garage carried on selling petrol until recent years and is now a motoring centre (see p.114).

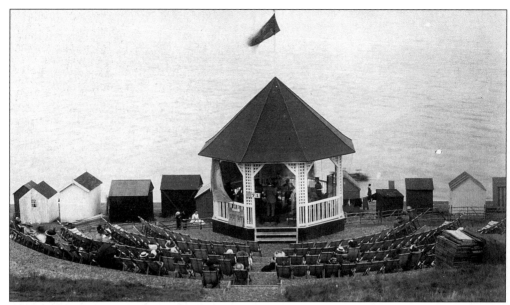

The bandstand, with the Whitstable Town Band practising, probably for a forthcoming Regatta Day, in the late '30s. It was built before 1914 by Mr Porter from a George Reeves' design. It has been gone now for some considerable time. Situated on Tankerton Slopes it was a very popular local venue.

The Boating Lake in Seasalter, developed by Mr Dick Scammell from a small dyke that crossed the golf course and ran into this lake. Many youngsters, the author included, enjoyed this lake with its rowing boats, canoes and paddle boats. It was filled-in during the 1960s and until recently, was the site for Whitstable Squash Rackets Club.

The Plough public house in St Johns Road at Swalecliffe on the old road from Whitstable to Herne Bay, in 1935. The old building seen here was demolished in 1938, the site becoming the car park and forecourt of the new building. In 1990 Thorley Taverns of Thanet were the owners and renamed it Eddery's after the famous jockey.

Chestfield and Swalecliffe Halt, c. 1940, showing a steam train in the station on the southern line to London. The road under the bridge leads to Swalecliffe, the road right leads to Chestfield. Cars and bicycles could park where they liked.

Side roads are always of interest to Whitstable natives, but some roads, like this one, were link roads. This picture, taken in 1932, shows South Street, which joins a part of Tankerton to Chestfield, mainly flanked by houses and farms.

This deserted road from a photograph taken in the 1940s is Douglas Avenue, which runs between Old Bridge Road, at the bottom of the hill, and Bellvue road at the top. The Sir William Nottridge School is situated on Bellvue Road.

Clare Road in Tankerton was a short cut from Tower Parade to Whitstable railway station.

A general view from Chestfield and Swalecliffe Halt, with a roundabout to the right. Left leads you to Herne Bay and Thanet; right, back to Whitstable and beyond and straight across, to Chestfield and Canterbury.

Taken in 1937 from Tankerton Circus, this photograph shows Tankerton Road heading towards Swalecliffe. The motor car is still not in everyone's price range but the types are more varied, with saloon and sports cars in view.

Looking at the Circus from Tankerton Road in the early 1940s. The Tankerton Circus Pharmacy is on the corner and to this day remains as such.

Looking the other way to the Circus, 1940s. George Fitt Motors is on the right hand side, at the back of the Marine Hotel along the sea front.

George Fitt Motors Ltd incorporating a taxi office with 'Open and Closed' cars for hire. Can this be right, £45 for the car on the left? The many petrol pumps meant a good turn round of customers. The garage was the starting point of trade in the Tankerton community and an important part of its history. Starting in 1919 with two employees, Fitt's expanded its premises to Faversham, Herne Bay and Margate. Notice the heavy spoked artillery-type wheels on the cars in the forecourt.

Tankerton Amusement Arcade at No. 1a Tower Parade, shortly after it opened in 1933. Owner Mr William Glover, the author's grandfather, is on the right facing us. Notice the amusement machines, especially the punch ball to the left, the human analyst next to the little girl, and the large weighing machine, far right.

Outside the arcade. No. 1 is Funland featuring Professor Domenyo, famous Egyptian palmist! The people behind the pin ball machines are, from left to right, Emma Akhurst, Gwen Austin with Ciss Glover and Bill Akhurst, daughter and son-in-law, to be, of William Glover.

East Cliffe at Tankerton, by Priest & Sow corner, in between Tankerton Road and Swalecliffe shops. Seen here are the small shops called Cliff Stores, incorporating a tea shop and garden, with people relaxing in the sun. Swalecliffe sea front is to the left.

Ye Old Sportsman public house dates back to 1840. The present building was built in 1890 after the inn was sold to Shepherd Neame, who continue as brewers to the present day. On 27 September 1940 a German Junkers 88 bomber crashed nearby on Graveney Marsh and soldiers dashed out of the pub to engage in a mini battle with the enemy.

Faversham Road, from Joy Lane, with the Sportsman in the far distance to the left, 1946. The motor cars pictured are Austins and Morrises and there are people camping on the site.

The Blue Anchor Caravan Park in Seasalter, late 1940s. The caravan holiday was becoming increasingly popular around Whitstable and Seasalter.

Old Chestfield Barn, now a licensed restaurant, is to the left, with Chestfield Golf Club house to the right. Reputed to date back to the fourteenth century the club house may be one of the oldest buildings in the country.

Interior of the old Tythe Barn, retaining its original look, but becoming tea rooms in the '30s and a restaurant from the '50s. The artifacts and relics go hand in hand with the old expression 'Lang mae ye lum reek', meaning 'long may your chimney smoke'.

The final photographs in this section show the devastation caused by the bombs and mine dropped by German bombers during the early years of the Second World War on Whitstable This one shows the rubble and fencing immediately in front of damaged buildings at the rear o Regents Street after a raid on 13 August 1940.

Regent Street after a huge mine was dropped on 11 October 1941.

A policeman inspects the damage caused by a mine that was dropped in Victoria Street.

More damage in Victoria Street. The houses to the right, with lock up garages, seem relatively undamaged, unlike the road to the left.

Tankerton did not escape the bombings of 1941 and this image shows Pier Avenue at its worst. Newton Road was also hit.

Pictures of bomb damage were witheld from publication during the war in case they assisted the enemy. This is Pier Avenue again.

Five
Up to 1970

A close up of the Bear and Key Hotel in 1969. The present massive facade was built around the 1870s. Well known for its good food, drink and accommodation, it continues to flourish to this day.

Harbour Street looking down towards Ludgate Hill, c. 1960. On the far right was the Lord Nelson public house, dating back to 1860. By 1894 the old building was knocked down and the present one erected. A decline in its condition forced closure in 1981. Furthest left is No. 24, now a junk shop; at No. 15 is John's Cafe and the weather-boarded shops are Nos 12 and 13, C.A. Liggins, electrical contractors; at No. 11 are Grays, builders merchants, who are still there today.

A 1960s view of Harbour Street, showing the restricted car parking spaces in this one-way system. Duffy's the butchers, right, is at No. 41 with Blaxland Farm Shop at Nos 39 and 40. Further along the road, R.W. Horne's newsagents occupies No. 43. Davey's the outfitters occupy Nos 44 and 45, just before the white building. To the right was V.C. Jones, fish fryers, at No. 25. The Lord Nelson can be seen in the distance, with an Ind Coope sign.

During the 1960s and early '70s No. 2a Albert Street, off Harbour Street was the premises of R.E. Glover, motor cycle sales and repairs, (the author's father). The scooter outside is a Vespa and the motor cycle a Triumph speed twin and sidecar.

The above premises also included parking facilities to the side and another property, far left. A Hudson auto cycle is parked in the road next to a Riley motor car. A Yamaha main agent for a number of years, Mr Glover also had a spares shop at 24 Harbour Street just out of picture to the right. In the '70s the business changed and became an industrial paint shop. The buildings have now been pulled down and the land redeveloped.

Borstal Hill Mill by the 1960s had become a fully licenced restaurant with chalet-type accommodation. The buildings were brightened up and it became a very popular place to visit.

Whitstable Bowling Club in the grounds of The Castle at Tankerton was formed in 1936. This is a 1960s view with the trees and shrubs in front of The Castle, forming a beautiful backdrop.

A view of Saddleton Road, just before 1970, showing the 2nd Whitstable Sea Scouts Mexican Band entry for the carnival. This was a regular starting point and to the left is Green Lane (out of picture). The tall building on the right is 11a Brenda House.

A late 1960s scene. Luckhurst & Son, general stores in Old Bridge Road, was run by father and son Eric and Michael Luckhurst from 1960 until 1973 when the business was sold. Originally, around 1918, Eric's father Silbert, and Edward Andrews, a builder and silent partner, traded as Andrews & Luckhursts from 45 Oxford Street. It later became Ron Willis the newsagents. Belmont Road flats can be seen on the left.

Classed as the 'Oldest Railway Bridge in the World' and arching over Old Bridge Road (once Church Road) by the station, this bridge was constructed in the late 1820s to carry the Whitstable-Canterbury railway line. It was finally demolished in 1969 for redevelopment.

The road leading from the other side of the railway station along Railway Avenue and Teynham Road, leading to Castle Road, 1960s. This bridge, a bit further along the line, came down shortly after the one above.

Dramatic moments after the demolition of the bridge had begun. A man inspects the unfinished work.

Another sad scene taken while the bulldozer driver had a break. Despite its age, the well made bridge did not give up easily.

An aerial view of the Hotel Continental, a very popular hotel. This scene is taken from a picture card printed for the owners, with an advertisement on the reverse.

The full magnificence of the Marine Hotel in Tankerton in the 1960s. In the early days of 1926 Mr George Fitt could only have imagined its potential. The building to the right was added on and the whole has now been converted to flats. In the far distance is Cliff Dene House.

Cliff Dene House along Tankerton Parade. The house has been used as a Methodist Home for the Aged since 1946. The Tankerton Hotel is further along the road.

The Blue Anchor Hotel in Seasalter along the Faversham Road, in 1955. The premises had, during the eighteenth century been called in turn the Crown, Rose and Crown, and the Anchor. It was rebuilt around 1900 and later became a popular Whitbread house for holidaymakers.

Looking into the Harbour from the East Quay, 1961. The area has been redeveloped and changes continue to occur. Notice the charming castellated building by Ludgate Hill in the background.

The putting green and tea gardens, situated opposite The Castle in Tankerton, were very popular recreational facilities for young and old, holidaymakers and locals alike, in the 1960s, but have now closed.

The promenade from the west at Tankerton. Photographed just before the swingboats were to disappear. The Savoy Restaurant is well marked. The Continental is to the left, with smart looking beach chalets on the right. The tea rooms are long gone.

THE SLOPES, TANKERTON

L 2328

A 1957 view of the steps leading up to Tankerton Slopes. The children, all wearing similar clothes, seem to be marching along; perhaps they are part of a school trip!

A splended 1960s view at Priest & Sow corner in Tankerton. The unusual name may come from an Anglo-Saxon expression. The road heading towards us leads to Tankerton sea front; the road to the right goes towards Swalecliffe.

The Broadway at Swalecliffe, leading from the road in the top picture. The petrol pumps are on the frontage of Quinney's Auto Services, today at 107 Herne Bay Road. The traffic seems fairly light for the 1960s. The Broadway stores and Martin's fisheries occupy Nos 89 and 90, respectively.

A picture postcard from 1964, showing the approach to Seaview Holiday Camp for caravans, along Colewood Road in Swalecliffe. Kite Farm Camps Ltd is indicated left.

The caravan, as popular as ever, is shown again in this 1950s view of Bay View Holiday Camp at Swalecliffe, a smaller site than Seaview (seen in the distance). The holidaymakers gather outside to have their picture taken.

The first of a selection of pictures taken by the photographer Douglas West, featuring various scenes of the 1953 flood. The flood occured when the sea wall was breached in the late evening of 31 January. This is Nelson Road with people being rescued by rowing boats.

The High Street was flooded with some three feet of water in parts; many people stand in shop doorways. Smith & Sons the bakers are at No. 69; No. 73 is C.W. George, barber, with Pearks Ltd next door.

Middle Wall, with people being rescued by rowing boats. The Wall Tavern public house is facing, with a white wall. This was Whitstable's worst flooding, but new sea defence walls have been built to ensure that this was the last such occurrence!

The Corner Shop at No. 15 Beech Walk, down which the men are heading. The main road, where the car is partially submerged, is Island Wall.

The flooding continues down Marine Parade with Tower Amusements evident at No. 1a. The water level at this point was not so high and the road is clear going towards The Castle. Although much property was damaged and destroyed, and many animals died, amazingly no human lives were lost.

To conclude this chapter I have included a view of the frozen sea on 14 January 1963. This shows Reeves Beach with fishermen's huts behind. The Neptune public house and *Vigilant* training ship are in clear view. This was the last big freeze of the sea around Whitstable.

Six

Recent Years

This photograph, from the *Kentish Gazette*, shows the 1979 Whitstable Regatta in full flow, complete with stalls, a fair, competitions and entertainment, all to be followed by an evening fireworks display. An escapologist plays centre stage in a mock up airplane. Having been lifted by crane from the cordened-off area, he successfully escaped from shackles, amazing his enthralled audience. Events like this on the Slopes have taken place every year since 1792, excepting the war years, usually on the first weekend in August. Sea sports events, so popular earlier in the century, have now ceased.

Apples car clinic, on the site of the original Long Reach filling station; to the left was Boon's Cafe by the Borstal Hill roundabout. The Headway Glazing building is on the far right. This busy crossroads for traffic to London, Canterbury and Thanet, has kept the site popular for the motorists' needs during the years.

Looking down Borstal Hill with Grimthorpe Avenue to the left, No. 10, on the corner, was built over two hundred years ago. This house has recently undergone major improvements, and looks very stylish again today.

Canterbury Road with the Two Brewers public house on the left. The present publican is Mick Queen who took over from Mrs Hollis in 1996. On the right hand side is the entrance to Forge Lane. Noah's Ark public house can be seen down the road with the sign on the furthest side wall.

The Oxford. Although the Bingo Hall had taken over from the cinema in the late '70s, films were still being shown there, alternating with bingo, until 1984. A recent late 1980s, early '90s film revival with better films on bigger budgets was, alas, not enough to restore the Oxford to its former glory.

A busy Whitstable High Street scene, looking up the town in the 1990s. Far left at No. 49 is the Cafe Bar and Kebab House takeaway; at Nos 51 and 53 is Stead and Simpson, shoe shop, with the Oxfam shop at No. 55; next door is Victoria Wine at No. 57; far right at No. 56 is Mackay's clothes shop. The National Westminster Bank occupies No. 58, along with Woolleys the shoe shop (since the 1930's) and, at No. 60 is Your Choice clothes shop, which had been Currys in the '70s and '80s.

The ever-changing businesses in the High Street. On the far left is Oyster Dry Cleaners at No. 108, next door was a fish shop in 1996 but in 1997 became AD 3000 Mobile Phone and Accessories. No. 104 has been Play House theatre since the late '80s, it was previously the Congregational Church Hall which moved to Middle Wall. Furthest right is Arminius (Ship Centurian) public house; interestingly the name is a Latin word for the 'God of Strength' and was added by Armin Birks who, with his wife Janet, has been the licencee since 1995. Next door is Whitstable Stationers at Nos 107 and 109. Family firm, Herbert's Cycles at Nos 103 and 105 has been there since 1939, previously occupying No. 3 Canterbury Road as wireless dealers.

This scene looking down the town shows, furthest right, ladies and gentleman's hairstylist at No. 97, next Pirie and Cavender's bookshop (since 1960s) which was originally The Queens Head inn. At No. 93 is Copperfields, general store, and Brian's, fruiterers occupies No. 91 opposite. Further down the road, occupying the tallest building, is the Salvation Army.

Present businesses include: furthest left Pets Pantry at No. 76, (showing theatre and concert tickets for sale); beyond the Salvation Army Hall is Ward and Partners Estate Agents at No. 74. The National Westminster Bank occupies Nos 78 and 80; No. 82 is the Chuffa Train Museum and, at No. 84, is Holdens the Jewellers (they had occupied No. 67 from the turn of the century). Opposite, furthest right: Dillnotts, bakers at No. 77; No. 75a Stuart's dry cleaners, next door, East Kent Models and at Nos 69 and 71, William Hill, bookmakers.

A recent view looking towards the Duke of Cumberland Hotel, shows W.J. Cox and Sons, stationers at No. 37 to the left of Michael Knowles Health Shop. At Nos 33 and 35 is Boots the chemist (previously Arthur Collar); Knowles Amusements take up Nos 29 and 31; Courts furniture shop is at Nos 21 and 23 (the tall building). On the other side from the far left: No. 50 Whites of Kent ladies shop, Somerfields, standing back from the road, used to be the Regal cinema, J.C. Rooks, the butcher, on the corner at No. 42, previously International Stores.

An up-to-date picture of Wheelers Oyster Bar at No. 8 High Street, once a family business and very popular for the seafood lover. The present managers of the Sheperd Neame Duke of Cumberland are Mr and Mrs Ripley who took over from Mrs Cunningham and Judith Baker in 1996. On the right is the Bear and Key Hotel, Mrs Sandy Clarke is the present landlady who took over from Mark and Karen Topsell. The Oyster Fishery restaurant can be seen in Horsebridge Road in the building originally used for the oyster industry. The sign on the wall reads 'Royal Free Fishers and Dredgers - incorporated 1793'.

118

A recent view looking down Ludgate Hill. On the left is The Punch Tavern (since 1958) which, although closed at the time of writing, is shortly to be reopened after the existing premises have been extended and refurbished by Mr John Kray. It was originally called The Railway Inn. Many of the side roads to the left down Harbour Street have been made into pedestrian walkways. The building to the right, along the sea wall, is Whitstable Marine Boats Sales and Service. The one-way system now includes the road to the left.

Looking down Harbour Street with, furthest left: Jan Grier, fancy clothes shop at No. 32 and Antoniou Hair Stylist at No. 31, here for many years. The Tudor Tearooms are further along. Furthest right is Shapla Tandoori Restaurant at No. 36, next door to the Harbour Street Arcade at Nos 37 and 38, which used to be Palais de Luxe cinema. Beyond the side road is No. 39, The Clothes Horse. The shop further down with the balcony is Birdies Restaurant at No. 41 and the building facing is Chatterbox tea rooms.

Along Old Bridge Road still stands Whitstable railway station, proudly showing its ticket machines. Looking virtually unchanged, but with no name above the frontage, this view dates from the late 1980s.

A view from the station on Old Bridge Road. The oldest railway bridge used to stand where the road bears to the right. Somehow its removal makes the road look very bare and many still regret the removal of this important piece of history.

Whitstable Harbour in the 1980s. Still a busy area for shipping, it hasn't lost any of its character and magic. The view speaks for itself.

The Whitstable Oyster and Fishery Exhibition at the harbour was opened in 1993 in response to popular demand for a record of the past. Mr John Bayes, owner of the Seasalter Shell Fish Company on the East Quay from 1986, set up the exhibition. The company was previously called the Seasalter and Ham Oyster Co. The exhibition was enlarged and refurbished in 1995 to cater for the ever increasing number of visitors eager to learn about Whitstable's most famous industry.

The Old Neptune public house as it is today. One of Whitstable's most famous drinking houses has had a face lift, but hasn't lost any of its old charm and character. Ms Allison Tapperden has been the landlady since 1992.

The old site of the Gorrell Tank. The Old Steam Packet public house, shown to the right, is now the Whitstable and District Angling Social Club. Notice the stands that are used for Whitstable market day, held in the car park every Thursday and still very popular with locals and visitors alike. The road alongside the houses shown is Cromwell Road.

Another view taken recently of Tower Parade. At No. 11 on the corner is Moby Dick, aquarium shop; next door is a private house, with Beth Saida, the Christian bookshop at No. 9. Next is Tower Cars, a local taxi firm at No. 8 with, nearest right, P.J. State-Side, Custom bikes. This later changed to Bits and Bobs, but sadly the premises are once again vacant. Opposite and facing is the building of 2-4 Tankerton Road general store.

A view to the right of the buildings in the top picture, with, from right to left: No. 1a Numark pharmacy (previously Tower Amusements). Notice the modern upper storey added for accommodation purposes. Then No. 1 Custom Video (a sign of the times) with the New World Chinese takeaway at No. 2; No. 3a is now Franks barber shop. The private house to the left is just before the gap that, regretably, was never developed and consequently shows much neglect.

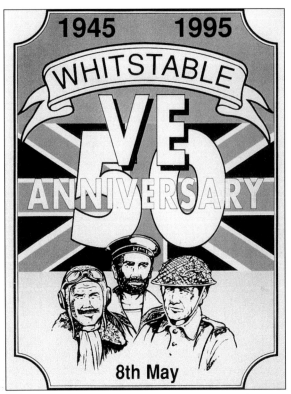

To commemorate the Golden Anniversaries of the end of the Second World War, Judy Baker of Boulevard Antiques, 139 Tankerton Road, published these two postcards in 1995 of VE Day on 8 May and VJ Day on 15 August 1945. Pictured are the Army, Navy and Royal Air Force in this most effective tribute from Whitstable town.

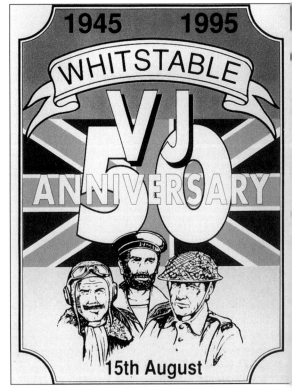

Seven
A Light Hearted Look!

The early years of the twentieth century saw the introduction of comic postcards. This final chapter features an appealing selection of these now rare cards portraying Whitstable. Those from the early 1900s and '20s illustrate light hearted views with self-explanatory captions. The 1950s and '60s saw a more saucy postcard being produced and these remain popular with the tourist, right up to the present day.

Whitstable – The Beach

We're finding all the quiet spots at Whitstable.

"Love all."

At Whitstable & Tankerton.